Reader, our warning is plain,
Laughing can give you a pain.
This silly collection
Might cause an infection
And seriously tickle your brain.

Old King Cole ☆ Doctor Foster ☆ Cool Queen Wence
Humpty Dumpty ☆ Bendy Burglar ☆ Incey Wincey ☆ Silly Sand

Really Frilly

YUM!

am the Man ☆ Johnny Stout ☆ Little Bo-Peep ☆ The Queen
Mary, Mary ☆ The Deadly Dinner Ladies ☆ Greedy Green Martian

 # CONTENTS

POTTY PONY POEM

I had a little pony,
His name was Dapple-Grey.
He seemed a little lonely,
I invited him to stay.

He sat down at my table,
He would not go away.
I moved into the stable,
Now all I eat is hay.

Dapple, stop this horseplay,
I've asked you lots of times,
Wrapped up in my duvet
With my *Seriously Silly Rhymes*.

DING DONG PONG

Ding dong bell
What's that funny smell?
It's worse than cheese
And slightly mouldy peas.
I have no doubt
It's little Johnny Stout
Who hasn't bathed in years,
Or washed behind his ears,
Or even used shampoo
Since 1992.

GREEDY GREEN MARTIAN

A greedy green Martian named Lars
Was sick of the sweets in the stars.
   He prayed every day
   For a huge Milky Way,
Then he flew off to Earth for a Mars.

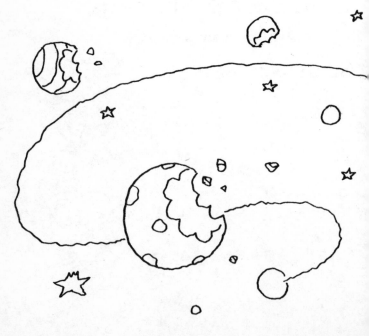

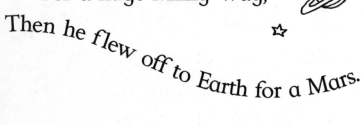

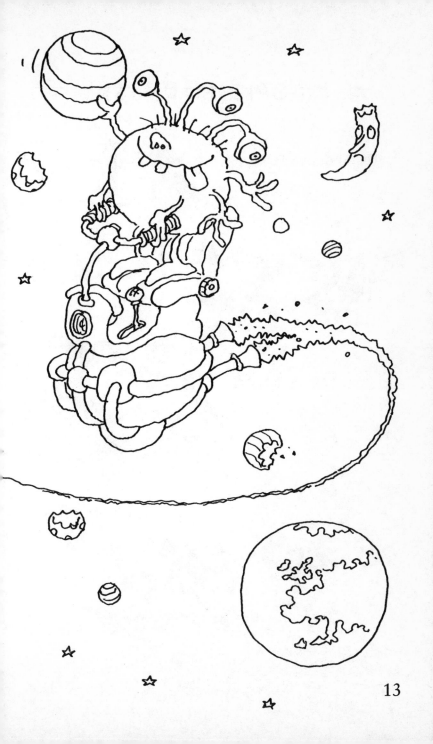

MAGPIE MADNESS

One for sorrow,

Two for a joke,

Three for a girlie,

Four for a bloke,

Five to get lucky,

Six to get broke,

Seven for some peanuts
And a can of Coke.

SEE-SORE SONG

Seesaw, Margery Daw,
Johnny will need a big plaster.
Margery Daw is twelve stone four.
It's what you might call a disaster.

TWINKLE WRINKLE

Twinkle, twinkle, my old Pa
Is so wrinkly (so's my ma).
Up above his vintage car,
Drifts the smoke of his old cigar.
Twinkle, twinkle, dear old Pa,
Your teeth are twinkly in their jar.

DIN DIN SONG

What is for dinner?
Ask the great bells of Pinner.
Oranges and lemons,
Say the bells of St Clement's.

What is for afters?
Ask the bells of Jakarta.

Old boots in butter,
Say the bells of Calcutta.

That really is yucky,
Say the bells of Kentucky.

Boiled bats and bananas?
Say the bells of the Bahamas.
I feel slightly ill,
Say the bells of Notting Hill.

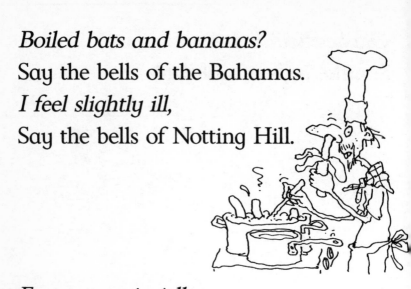

Frogspawn in jelly,
Say the big bells of Delhi.
Pass me a bucket,
Say the bells of Nantucket.

Steamed socks and snails,
Say the old bells of Wales.
Please bring me the bill,
Say the bells of West Hill.

WILD WEE WILLIE

Wee Willie Winkie, driving us
   bananas
Upstairs and downstairs in his
   pink pyjamas.

Rap and disco, pop and rock.

SILLY SIMON

Simple Simon met a fireman
Going to a fire.
Says Simple Simon to the fireman,

Says the fireman to Simple Simon,
"I wouldn't mind a hose."
Says Simple Simon to the fireman,

Says the fireman to Simple Simon,
"Hurry up then, mate.
The fire's getting hotter
And we're going to be too late."

Says Simple Simon to the fireman,

Says the fireman to Simple Simon,

You're such a simple bloke.
It's your house that's on fire,
And it's just gone up in smoke.

I NEED SOME KNITTED KNICKERS

Baa baa, black sheep,
Have you any wool?
I want some knitted knickers,
I think they'd look quite cool.

Some for my granny,
Some for my mum.

And some would be
Just for me
To cover up my bum.

I HAD A CUTE CHAMELEON

I had a cute chameleon;
He was my favourite pet.
He ate some grass and turned bright
    green;
I took him to the vet.

The vet said, "Oh, you simpleton,
Why don't you use your head?
Chameleons are camouflaged."
I instantly turned red.

SILLY DILLY

Lavender's brown, dilly dilly,
Lavender's green.

Make up your mind, silly silly,
What do you mean?

Lavender's black, dilly dilly,
Lavender's pink.

Will you decide, silly silly,
What do you think?

Lavender's red, dilly dilly,
Lavender's blue.

Why not admit, silly silly,
You don't have a clue?

EGGSCELLENT!

Little Miss Muffet
Mixed up an omelette
And started to feel unwell.
Just for a joke, she'd thrown out the
yolk,
But eaten up all of the shell.

CHRISTMAS CRACKERS

Christmas is over, the geese are
    getting thin.
Please don't poke the pimple on the
    old man's chin.
If you poke his pimple, it really is
    quite simple,
He'll tie you up with tinsel and fling
    you in the bin.

SNOTTY SPOTTY SONG

Ladybird, ladybird,
Feeling quite grotty.
Got measles from weasels,
Which made her dots spotty.

Got a bug from a pug,
Which made her all snotty.

Sat down on her potty,
Which stuck to her botty.

SPEEDY WEEDS

The coach of a top squad from Leeds
Said, "You play like a big bunch of
weeds."
He placed a small rocket
In every back pocket,
Then they ran at remarkable speeds.

39

A TINY BUM HUM

Ring-a-ring o' roses,
We all want studs in our noses,
A tattoo! A tattoo!
Of roses on my bum.

RIDE A BIG SKATEBOARD

Ride a big skateboard to Banbury
    Cross
To see a fat lady in a white Porsche.
She never stops talking although she's
    alone,
Yackety-yak on her hands-free phone.

NUTTY NATIONAL ANTHEM

God save our gracious queen,
Wrap her in polythene,
And margarine.
She is mysterious,
Strangely delirious,
And oh-so serious
Like an old sardine.

SERIOUSLY FRILLY RHYME

We three kings of Orient are,
Searching the East for an
    extra-large bra.
It's for our camel, the lumpy old
    mammal,
The one with the giant cigar.

Oh-oh, bra of wonder, bra of might,
Be sure her humps are not too tight.
Don't be silly, that's far too frilly
To keep her warm right through
the night.

ALL ABOUT
THE AUTHOR

Mr Laurence Anholt
Is what the author's called.
His hair is longish at the back
But on the top he's bald.

He sits at his computer
In shirts of cornflower blue.
He broke his favourite teacup
But mended it with glue.

He creeps out in the dead of night
And stares up at the moon.
He plays his music far too loud,
And dances like a loon.

ALL ABOUT
THE ILLUSTRATOR

ARTHUR'S
SHED

Let's visit Arthur Robins now,
We'll find him in this shed.
It's full of junk and rather small,
You'll have to mind your head.

This is the desk where Arthur works,
Here is his comfy chair.
And in it is the man himself –
Please try hard not to stare.

Hush! He's started drawing now.
I can't believe my eyes!
He's working on those silly books
Which won a major prize.*

* Smarties Gold Award

47

SERIOUSLY SILLY
RHYMES and STORIES

Laurence Anholt ☆ Arthur Robins

All priced at £3.99

Seriously Silly books are available from all good bookshops,
or can be ordered direct from the publisher:
Orchard Books, PO BOX 29, Douglas IM99 1BQ
Credit card orders please telephone 01624 836000
or fax 01624 837033
or e-mail: bookshop@enterprise.net for details.

To order please quote title, author and ISBN
and your full name and address.
Cheques and postal orders should be
made payable to 'Bookpost plc'.
Postage and packing is FREE within the UK
(overseas customers should add £1.00 per book).

Prices and availability are subject to change.